HIP-HOP

Hip-Hop

Chris Brown

James Hooper

Mason Crest Publishers

Chris Brown

FRONTIS Though still a teenager, Chris Brown has hit the music scene with a bang. And there's much more to come.

PRODUCED BY 21ST CENTURY PUBLISHING AND COMMUNICATIONS, INC.

EDITORIAL BY HARDING HOUSE PUBLISHING SERVICES, INC.

MASON CREST PUBLISHERS INC.
370 Reed Road
Broomall, Pennsylvania 19008
(866)MCP-BOOK (toll free)
www.masoncrest.com

Printed in Malaysia.

9 8 7 6 5 4 3 2

Library of Congress Cataloging-in-Publication Data

Hooper, James, 1957–
    Chris Brown / by James Hooper.
       p. cm. — (Hip-hop)
    Includes bibliographical references (p.   ) and index.
  ISBN 1-4222-0177-5
    1. Brown, Chris, 1989–   —Juvenile literature. 2. Rap musicians—United States—Biography—Juvenile literature. I. Title. II. Series.
  ML3930.B865H66 2007
  782.421649092—dc22
  [B]   2006014899

Publisher's notes:
- All quotations in this book come from original sources, and contain the spelling and grammatical inconsistencies of the original text.

- The Web sites mentioned in this book were active at the time of publication. The publisher is not responsible for Web sites that have changed their addresses or discontinued operation since the date of publication. The publisher will review and update the Web site addresses each time the book is reprinted.

Contents

Hip-Hop Timeline

1974 Hip-hop pioneer Afrika Bambaataa organizes the Universal Zulu Nation.

1988 *Yo! MTV Raps* premieres on MTV.

1970s Hip-hop as a cultural movement begins in the Bronx, New York City.

1985 *Krush Groove,* a hip-hop film about Def Jam Recordings, is released featuring Run-D.M.C., Kurtis Blow, LL Cool J, and the Beastie Boys.

1970s DJ Kool Herc pioneers the use of breaks, isolations, and repeats using two turntables.

1979 The Sugarhill Gang's song "Rapper's Delight" is the first hip-hop single to go gold.

1986 Run-D.M.C. are the first rappers to appear on the cover of *Rolling Stone* magazine.

1970   1980   1988

1976 Grandmaster Flash & the Furious Five pioneer hip-hop MCing and freestyle battles.

1986 Beastie Boys' album *Licensed to Ill* is released and becomes the best-selling rap album of the 1980s.

1970s Break dancing emerges at parties and in public places in New York City.

1982 Afrika Bambaataa embarks on the first European hip-hop tour.

1988 Hip-hop music annual record sales reaches $100 million.

1970s Graffiti artist Vic pioneers tagging on subway trains in New York City.

1984 *Graffiti Rock,* the first hip-hop television program, premieres.

1993 Rapper Snoop Dogg's album *Doggystyle* is the first debut album to hit the music charts at number one.

2006 Queen Latifah becomes the first hip-hop artist to receive a star on the Hollywood Walk of Fame.

1989 DJ Jazzy Jeff & The Fresh Prince become the first hip-hop artists to win a Grammy Award.

2003 Rapper Eminem becomes the first hip-hop artist to win an Academy Award.

2005 Hip-hop artist Kanye West appears on the cover of *Time* magazine.

1989 Rap is added as a new category to the *Billboard* charts.

1997 East Coast rapper Notorious B.I.G. (aka Biggie Smalls) is murdered.

2004 First National Hip-Hop Political Convention is held in Newark, New Jersey.

1989   **2000**   **2006**

1990s Hip-hop emerges in Europe.

1996 West Coast rapper Tupac Shakur is shot and killed.

2005 Rapper Will Smith opens the Philadelphia Live 8 concert as part of 10 simultaneous concerts held worldwide to bring attention to the extreme poverty in Africa.

1989 First gangsta rap album, *Straight Outta Compton*, is released by N.W.A.

2001 The hip-hop political action group, Hip-Hop Summit Action Network, is founded by Russell Simmons.

2006 The Smithsonian Institute National Museum of American History announces the creation of a new hip-hop exhibition scheduled to open in three to five years.

1992 Dr. Dre's album *The Chronic* is released; it redefines West Coast rap.

Chris has taken the word "yo" and given it new importance. His song "Yo" brought him the attention of the music industry and fans, and sent his career soaring. Soon he was appearing on such TV shows as *New Year's Rockin' Eve*.

‹1›

Yo!

"**W**hen you say 'yo' to a girl, whether it be at an amusement park or the mall, [it can be] offensive," Chris Brown told MTV. "It's like, 'Yo, yo, yo,' and the girl will be like, 'What?' . . . But I try to flip it and make it seem like that's the only thing I *could* say, like, 'Yo, you took my breath away.'"

Chris Brown is only a teenager—but he's already a hot star in the world of hip-hop music. His single, "Yo," and its video helped launch his shining star straight up to the top of the music industry's sky.

According to the Chris Brown Web site:

"**When Chris Brown says 'yo' it's as if he gives new meaning, new depth and whole new feeling to the word. Chris'[s] vocals are fresh and invited, soulful and soaring. He wraps his emotions around each and every lyric and adds the right amount of passion, fun and swagger at just the right time.**"

The video that goes along with the song, which is co-directed by Chris himself, opens with Chris in the role of a worker at an upscale sneaker store, running late for work. On his way, he becomes distracted by a beautiful young woman and starts to follow her, trying to grab her attention by pulling out all his moves (with a little help from his boys).

"I try to bring a little swagger to it," Chris told MTV. "We do our little dance and I just sing the whole song to her and let her know that I'm not the typical guy. . . . I'm trying to be a gentleman about it."

The video featured not just one but two songs by Chris; it cut from "Yo" to "Gimme That." Throughout the video, Chris's hot dance moves, what he calls "crumpin', poppin' and slottin,'" lights up the music. "I show a little more of the rugged, street part of the dancing," Chris said in the interview with MTV. "There's sort of a 'Rhythm Nation'-type feel with all-black suits on. You'll see like the Black Panther, the gasoline worker and me as a S.W.A.T. man. [It'll have] all different aspects. It's just crazy."

Chris's moves are an important part of his stardom. As young as he is, he's a shining example of what makes hip-hop so popular.

History of Hip-Hop

Hip-hop is America's very own child, a unique art form born of the **minority** cultures brought together within the United States. You could consider some of hip-hop's grandparents to be Jamaican and Hispanic music—but its oldest grandparents were raised on Africa's soil.

Back in the seventeenth, eighteenth, and nineteenth centuries, the people brought to America as slaves refused to give up their humanity. They clung to their identity and dignity through their faith, their love—and their music. They sang even within slavery's cruel grasp, and as they sang, they clapped and stamped, shouted and danced. Life's rhythms stirred their blood and gave them hope. For them, song, stories, prayer, and dance were a single thing. How could a person tell a story and not break into song? How could he sing and not begin to dance? How could he dance and not pray? The lives of these earliest African Americans were filled with sorrow and cruelty, but their faith in the spiritual world was strong. Rhythm was part of both their work and their worship; complaining about their lot in life and preaching their faith, dancing and singing, all blended together.

As the years went by, black Americans kept on dancing to life's beat. In African American churches, ministers' voices rose and fell, the

Angola's Capoeira is another influence on hip-hop. A combination of dance, music, and martial arts, Capoeira dates from Portuguese slave colonies. Slaveholders wouldn't allow their slaves to perform martial arts, but they could dance to their traditional rhythms.

Gospel and other forms of church music have influenced many music genres, including hip-hop. But it wasn't just the music that made a difference. The rhythm of the spoken word also found its way into different music styles.

pitch of their voices creating a rhythm that often burst into song. At the same time, the members of the choir might start shouting out their **testimonies** in the middle of a song, or the preacher might weave his preaching through the singers' music. Music, spoken words, clapping, swaying, all flowed together seamlessly.

But African American music wasn't kept inside church walls. It was also in the streets and dance halls. In the first half of the twentieth century, even white folk started listening to "the blues," music that came directly from the slaves' spirituals and chants. In the 1920s, jazz, yet another offspring of African American music, became popular across the United States. And then the blues and jazz got married and had their own child—rhythm and blues, or R&B. By now, this wasn't just black folks' music. White people were singing along, and R&B grew up to be America's most famous musical child: rock'n'roll.

During the 1960s, another musical marriage came along; **gospel** and R&B combined their religious and **secular** themes into "soul" music. The same word—soul—expressed African Americans' sense of pride and identity. Musician James Brown was a figurehead for this movement. He made people all across America stand up and take notice: black folks were proud of who they were. They were beautiful and strong—and their music helped make them that way.

The way James Brown blended blues, gospel, jazz, and country vocal styles made him one of the most influential musicians of the twentieth century—but James Brown didn't just sing. He also jumped; he stamped his feet; he fell to his knees; he swayed; he danced with his microphone; and he made rhythm more important than it had ever been. What's more, his music inspired yet another new form of American music—funk.

Compared to soul music, funk had fancier rhythms and simpler melodies. A typical funk song was just one or two short musical phrases, repeated over and over to the beat. Funk music was meant for dancing. You might say that after a whole long string of great grand-daddies and grandmas—slave songs and spirituals, the blues and jazz, R&B and rock'n'roll—funk was the mama that gave birth to hip-hop.

And you could probably say that Jamaican party music was the daddy. Two Jamaican **DJs**, Kool Herc and D.J. Hollywood, were the first to introduce America to a new party sound. Herc used two copies of the same record to turn a fifteen-second segment into a piece of music that went on and on, mixing back and forth between the two records, using the turntables as musical instruments. And while Herc was performing with turntables, he was also **emceeing**, using his microphone to mix in jokes and comments. Herc's musical parties became even more famous once they were recorded on cassette tapes and passed around, allowing other DJs to imitate his style.

When Kool Herc DJed, he extended the "breaks"—the parts where the percussion was the strongest—for as long as possible by using two

James Brown is one of the most important influences on music today. The "Godfather of Soul" mixed soul, gospel, jazz, and country music with his energetic gyrations to create a new musical form and a new type of entertainment.

turntables with double copies of the same record. The dancers who rocked out on the dance floor to the rhythm of these "breakbeats" became known as break-boys or b-boys; later still, they would be known as break-dancers. Their earliest moves—called the "drop" and the "in and out"—were influenced not only by the music's beat but also by moves from Asian martial arts and Latino dances. Graffiti was hip-hop's visual art; emceeing and DJing produced the rap; and b-boying was the dance.

In hip-hop's earliest days, the most important "performers" were the DJs. Using turntables to scratch and mix records, the DJs provided the sound that got the people onto the dance floor—and eventually brought hip-hop into the mainstream.

Once hip-hop hit the scene, New York City crowds began seeing b-boys bending their bodies into pretzel-like shapes on city corners. Break dancing began in clubs, but its energy could not be contained, and exhibitions like the one seen here became commonplace.

In hip-hop's early days, all these elements were braided as tight as a pigtail. Graffiti taggers were often b-boys, emcees, and DJs as well. At parties in New York City's South Bronx, graffiti artists sprayed their designs on a wall, a DJ spun and scratched on the black plastic discs, and the emcee got the crowd excited. Meanwhile, the b-boys were out on the dance floor, each one trying to do outdo the other with his moves.

Pretty soon, city kids throughout the Bronx were joining in. And then hip-hop traveled west and south, to cities on the West Coast and down South. You didn't need a lot of money to rap; all you needed was your voice and your hands. You didn't need fancy lessons to break-dance; all you needed was a flexible body and a sense of rhythm. You didn't need expensive art materials to make graffiti; all you needed was a can of spray paint and a subway car or a blank wall. Whether they were dancing, tagging, or rapping, city kids had found themselves a new way to express themselves. In a world where jobs and opportunities were scarce, where prejudice and violence were everyday realities, and where hope and dignity were hard to come by, hip-hop offered urban kids something new: a sense of pride and identity.

This brand-new world of music was still completely **spontaneous**, though. The only recordings were live **bootleg** tapes passed around from boom box to boom box. And then all that changed when the Sugarhill Gang released the first rap records. After that, all the rappers got busy making their own singles. And finally, for the first time, mainstream white America heard hip-hop come booming out of their radios.

While hip-hop's music was beating out across America's airways, break dancing was also jumping out of the city streets. By the 1980s, kids in small towns across rural America knew about moves like locking, popping, and the electric boogaloo. Even white kids were trying the moves.

After only a few years, hip-hop had grown up. Now it wasn't just something city kids were doing down in the streets of New York and Los Angeles, it had gone mainstream. You could hear hip-hop everywhere from commercials to white pop music. By 1988, the annual record sales of hip-hop music reached $100 million.

Chris Brown's Place in Hip-Hop

Hip-hop was born long before Chris Brown came along on May 5, 1989. Compared to the old-timers—folks like Grandmaster Flash and

Reverend Run—Chris is just a baby. Chris is taking his place in the hip-hop world, though. His hot moves, his street-slang raps, and his attitude all prove that he's a genuine child of hip-hop, a youngster who grew up listening to the real thing from the time he was little.

According to MTV, it's Chris's dance moves that are partly responsible for his growing popularity. "Brown's happy feet are so on-point," wrote an MTV reviewer, "he hardly had use for a **choreographer**." Chris explained to the interviewer:

> **"When they did single shots of everybody, it was all freestyle, everybody bringing their new style to the table. There was nothing really choreographed except the group dancing, when you see me and various other dancers doing it in unison. But every single other dance, with me, it was freestyling. I guess the spirit was in us. We was doing it."**

"Yo (Excuse Me Miss)" isn't Chris's only hit single. He has released a string of mid-tempo **ballads**, silky romantic songs that also pop with hip-hip rhythm. His lyrics are clever and intelligent, and already he's being compared to hip-hop star Usher, back when Usher was getting started. Other critics point out, though, that even Usher wasn't as successful back in his early days as Chris Brown has already become. Chris is no mere Usher wannabe, and while his voice may not yet have matured, his vocals are already so perfect that critics believe they will only soar higher with age.

Chris's songs are honest and revealing; they explore what it means to be a teenager who's beginning to explore the world of romance. On his Web site, he explained that his songs rely on his own sense of what "was hot and what was real." He said, "When I hear these songs, I feel something. I know I can relate to them. I take myself out of the artist box and I become an audience member and I critique myself."

This ability he has to sense how he will be perceived by his audience allows him to come across as mature and classy. On his Web site, he further explained:

> **"You don't want to come out too sexual. I'm young. I want to appeal to people my age as well as older people. This gives me time to grow with my audience**

Chris is perhaps best known for his carefully crafted dance moves. Young people all over the world imitate the energetic, smooth moves that help define Chris Brown, hip-hop star. Here he is shown performing on 2005's *New Year's Rockin' Eve*.

Though his career is still in its beginning stages, Chris has made huge steps toward becoming a hip-hop icon. He has learned from those who came before him and is using that knowledge to develop his own style.

so I can make that change when I'm about twenty. But for right now I don't wanna be too kiddie but I don't wanna be too grown."

Despite his young age, Chris insists on being taken seriously. "You know," he told MTV, "people see the video and they see the singer, but they don't really see the artist. They'll say, 'Oh, he's just dancing. He's just got a hot song right now,' but what they don't know is that the whole album is incredible." In other words, Chris Brown is more than just a couple of songs and some good dance moves. He sees himself as a whole lot more than just a kid who's had a run of luck. He's planning on a lifetime career.

THE OFFICIAL CHRIS BROWN POSTER SPECIAL!

Everything You Want To Know About Chris Brown!

ALL EXCLUSIVE Interviews & Hot Pix!

Go On The Set Of Yo!

INSIDE 16 GLORIOUS COLOR PULL-OUTS OF CHRIS!

Can You Be Chris's Crush?

WordUp! **WINTER 2006**
$4.99 USA $5.99 CANADA £2.75 U.K.

0 09281 01612 0

Win A Phone Call From Chris!

Chris readily acknowledges the influence other artists have had on his music. In the winter 2006 issue of *WordUp!* Chris discusses how artists such as Sam Cooke, Michael Jackson, and Aretha Franklin have affected his music.

Run It!

When Chris Brown was growing up in a small town called Tappahannock in Virginia, he was inspired by African American musicians like Michael Jackson, Sam Cooke, Stevie Wonder, Donnie Hathaway, Anita Baker, and Aretha Franklin. These stars shaped Chris's musical talents—and they proved to him that music was a path that could take him all the way to the top.

Michael Jackson

Born in 1958, Michael Jackson was already a star by the time he was five years old. In the 1960s, he and his four older brothers made the Jackson 5 a household word across America; when he was only thirteen, he launched his own solo career. Although in recent years his personal life has been marred with controversy and rumors, no one can argue with his professional success: his album *Thriller* is the best-selling album of all time, earning worldwide sales of $60 million, thirteen Grammys, and thirteen number-one singles. Jackson has been awarded numerous honors, including the World Music Award's Best-Selling Pop Male Artist of the Millennium. Michael Jackson is also a double-**inductee** into the Rock and Roll Hall of Fame (both as a solo artist and as a member of the Jackson 5).

Jackson's music is classified as pop—he took aspects of black music and made it mainstream, so that everybody in the entire world was singing along—but hip-hop influenced his style, and he in turn influenced many of the big-name hip-hop musicians. What's more, he brought break dancing to the entire world with his popping and locking, and especially his moonwalk. Most important, Michael Jackson taught Chris Brown that a black kid could grow up to be a superstar.

Sam Cooke

Before Michael Jackson ever came along, however, Sam Cooke had already proved what a young African American musician could accomplish. Born in 1931 and dead at the young age of thirty-three, Cooke began his musical career with his three siblings as a member of a quartet called the Singing Children. As a teenager, he was part of a gospel group called the Highway QCs, and at nineteen, he joined another group called the Soul Stirrers, where he achieved success and fame within the gospel community. In 1956, he released his first pop single, "Lovable," under the alias Dale Cooke, since at that time gospel fans did not want their stars singing secular music. No one could mistake Cooke's unique vocals, though, and soon he was singing under his own name.

As an R&B performer writing his own songs and achieving mainstream fame, Sam Cooke astonished the music industry in the 1960s. He went even further and founded his own record label (SAR Records), as well as a publishing imprint and a management firm. Like most R&B artists of his time, Cooke focused on singles; in all he had twenty-nine top-40 hits on the pop charts and even more on the R&B charts. He also wrote many of the most popular songs of all time, performed by other artists (and often uncredited to Cooke by the general public).

Cooke not only influenced Chris Brown while he was growing up in the early twenty-first century; Cooke also helped shape the entire modern music industry. Even people who have never heard one of his records have still heard his voice and phrasing if they have

Few people in the world are unaware of Michael Jackson and his influence on music. He is also responsible for bringing break dancing into the mainstream. Here he performs his famous "moonwalk" at the MTV Video Music Awards in 1995.

Sam Cooke was a music pioneer. He wrote his own songs, achieved widespread fame, and founded his own record label, publishing imprint, and management firm. Though he died in 1964, his musical influence continues in the work of Rod Stewart, Bruce Springsteen, and Chris Brown.

listened to any Rod Stewart, Simon and Garfunkle, James Taylor, Bruce Springsteen, Smokey Robinson, or Marvin Gaye. What's more, Cooke showed hip-hop artists that black musicians could use their talent to build an entire business career that extended beyond simply singing songs. Many of the greatest hip-hop stars—people like Usher, P. Diddy, and Mary J. Blige—have followed in Sam Cooke's footsteps, carving out influential careers for themselves that take them beyond the music industry. So when Chris looked to Sam Cooke as one of his heroes, he had one of the best role models of all time.

Stevie Wonder

Chris Brown has also pointed to Stevie Wonder as one of his inspirations. By doing so, Chris has yet again chosen from the best. Wonder has recorded more than thirty top-10 hits; he's won twenty-four Grammy awards (a record for a living artist), including one for lifetime achievement; and he has been inducted into both the Rock and Roll and Songwriters halls of fame. Blind since he was a baby, Stevie Wonder has let nothing hold him back. His record sales total more than 100 million units, and he has also written and produced for many other musicians. Amazingly **versatile**, Wonder plays the drums, the bass guitar, the congas, the piano, the harmonica, and keyboards. Critics consider him to be a musical genius. His style and innovations have influenced the music worlds of pop, R&B, and hip-hop, and Chris isn't the only hip-hop artist who looks to Stevie for inspiration. Mariah Carey, Kanye West, Alicia Keys, John Legend—as well as R&B musicians like Jay Kay, India.Arie, Musiq Soulchild, and Dru Hill—all list Stevie Wonder as one of the major influences on their careers.

Stevie Wonder has also shown that a successful musician has opportunities that lie beyond the music world. His commitment to various social and charitable issues has influenced the lives of many performers, especially in the world of hip-hop, where the brightest stars are doing their part to change the world for the better.

Donnie Hathaway

A soul musician famous for his duets with Roberta Flack, Donnie Hathaway helped shape the music of the 1970s. Like many modern African American musicians, fame came to him early, and he was offered professional opportunities before he had even graduated from college. His songs could be smooth and romantic, while others were

Stevie Wonder started his superstar musical career at an even younger age than Chris. At age twelve, he signed a record deal with Motown, a major music giant-maker. Stevie is a musical genius, playing several instruments and writing and producing mega-hits for himself and others.

fiery, social commentaries. Eventually, he was considered the greatest soul musician of the 1970s. Although his life was marred by depression (and he eventually took his own life in 1979, when he was only thirty-three), his influence continues to be felt today. Chris Brown is not the only young musician who counts Hathaway as one of the major influences on his work.

Anita Baker

In the 1980s, Anita Baker helped define a classy, refined brand of romantic soul. Her own music was shaped by R&B, jazz, gospel, and traditional pop; she proved that a black musician could pull from the best of all worlds and create a sound uniquely her own that appealed to mainstream America. The romance of her songs is one of the elements that shows up in Chris Brown's music as well.

Aretha Franklin

Dubbed both the "Queen of Soul" and "Lady Soul," Aretha Franklin helped transform gospel, soul, and R&B into mainstream music. After winning eighteen Grammys (including eleven for Best Female R&B Vocal Performance), she is the second-most honored female singer in Grammy history (after Alison Krauss). The state of Michigan declared her voice a natural wonder, and industry publications and media outlets like *Rolling Stone*, VH1, and *American Billboard* regard her as one of the best vocalists of all time. No matter what she sings, she fills it with gut-wrenching, honest emotion and conviction. It is this honesty that especially speaks to hip-hop artists like Chris Brown.

Making the Music His Own

Lots of people are inspired by musicians like Stevie Wonder and Aretha Franklin—but it takes something special to actually follow in their footsteps. Chris Brown is still too young for critics to judge where he'll end up, but he has had the courage to take those initial all-important steps.

In late 2005, he released his **debut** single "Run It!" The song was originally recorded without rapper Juelz Santana, but a rap by Santana was later added to the song in order to make it appeal to a wider audience, especially hip-hop fans. The song climbed the charts to the top 100, where it stayed for five weeks. It was also a big hit worldwide, peaking at number one on the Australian singles chart and debuting at number two in the United Kingdom.

"Queen of Soul," "Lady Soul": these are just two titles used to describe Aretha Franklin. She brings gospel, soul, and R&B into popular music. Her importance to the music industry is without question, as is her talent. Michigan even declared her voice a natural wonder.

Juelz Santana (born LaRon Louis James on February 18, 1984) is an African American and Dominican rapper from Harlem, who is best known for his featured contributions to hip-hop star Cam'ron's 2002 hits, "Oh Boy" and "Hey Ma." Like Chris, Juelz's career got under way when he was still just a kid; he began writing rhymes at the age of twelve. He was originally signed to Priority Records as one half of a duo called Draft Pick, and then, in 1998, he became a member of a hip-hop group called the Diplomats, whose members included Cam'ron, Jim Jones, and Freekey Zeekey.

Teaming up with Santana helped Chris's reputation in a number of ways; after all, Santana was voted number two in *Vibe*'s top-fifty sexiest rappers (behind T.I.). Like Santana, Chris is definitely considered hot by his female fans!

In 2005, Chris released his debut single, "Run It!" featuring Juelz Santana. The record brought Chris a worldwide audience and fans eager for more. Though Santana is sometimes controversial, his appearance on Chris's single didn't hurt sales.

Chris's first album also came out in late 2005. It climbed to number one on the *Billboard* R&B/Hip-Hop albums chart. In January, the album became platinum. With the success of the album and singles released from it, Chris's career was skyrocketing.

Santana, however, may be best known for taking a controversial stand after the September 11, 2001, terrorist attacks, when one of his raps included these words: "I worship the late prophet/The great Mohammed Omar Atta/For his courage behind the wheel of the plane." The media called Santana's lyrics "detestable," but Santana insisted that he "didn't say nothing bad about September 11th." In a press release, he said: "I just stated the fact of Atta's courage. A lot of people are not willing to do what he did, and that's the same way I feel about my Diplomat family. I'd do anything for them, and he did anything for what he believed in." Santana's reputation survived this blip on his screen, and his fame and popularity did Chris's debut album a lot of good.

The same year as the release of his debut single, Chris's self-titled debut album *Chris Brown* was released. The album went as far as number two on the *Billboard* Hot 200 albums chart, and it hit number one on the R&B/Hip-Hop albums chart. A month later, on January 12, 2006, the album was already certified **platinum**. The second single from the album, "Yo," also climbed the charts to number seven. More singles from the album followed, and Chris's career was off and running.

For any artist's career to succeed, he or she needs a good manager, someone who knows the ins and outs of the music business. Chris found his in Tina Davis, formerly with Def Jam Records—a giant in hip-hop music.

3

Learning the Business

Chris owes much of his style and inspiration to the all-time greatest black American musicians. In the practical business of launching a music career, however, he's in debt to two people: Tina Davis and Scott Storch. As his manager, Tina Davis helped Chris shape the day-to-day details of his career; and as his producer, Scott Storch made Chris's musical talent shine.

Tina Davis

Chris described to Urban Connectionz how his career first got under way:

> **"Well, I started singing when I was eleven, and from there, at the age of thirteen, I hooked up with some people in my area that had studios. . . . From there, they introduced me to some more people, and eventually**

we went to New York. In New York, they had a small production team, so I recorded like twelve songs. . . . Out of the blue, my production team called and said I had a meeting with Def Jam, so . . . I went in there and performed for the Senior Vice President of A&R, Tina Davis, and she liked me. She just gave me advice, and then she took me to perform for LA Reid, and he wanted to sign me. While Rocafella and Def Jam was doing their merger, Tina Davis got sprung from Def Jam, and she became my manager. She asked me if I wanted to shop for deals anywhere else because she had connections at some other places and . . . at the end of the day, I signed with Jive."

Tina Davis tells her side of the story to Pollstar:

"I picked Chris out of the seven acts because of his voice. When he came to my office, he was a little nervous. He performed for me, then I had him perform for a couple of people in the office. Each time, he got better. I gave him very little direction before we went to LA Reid. He just took this tiny bit of information . . . and turned it into a great performance. He blew everybody away in the room!"

Chris told Pollstar that he hadn't known what to expect from his first meeting with Davis.

"At first I thought the record label would be real big snobby people, like 'OK, sing, hurry up,' but she was real nice and down to earth. She told me her track record and who she's helped in the past. . . . I started to believe what she was saying, so by the time she took me to LA Reid I felt confident enough to perform my best. It was exciting."

Chris and his mother, Joyce Hawkins, moved to New Jersey to work with Davis on artist development. Davis continued their story in her interview with Pollstar:

"It was truly fate that Chris came in and I was left off [from Def Jam]. When he asked me to be his manager was when I decided to be a manager. We would sit down and talk about his ideas and his thoughts, and that's when I realized he's 100 percent an artist."

Together, Chris and Tina Davis were a winning combination with the skills the other needed to advance their careers. Now, all Chris needed to do was hook up with the right producer for his music.

Scott Storch

Born in 1973, Scott Storch is a Jewish American keyboardist, song-writer, and hip-hop producer. He grew up in Philadelphia, where he started playing piano when he was only four years old. Storch started his musical career as the keyboardist for an alternative hip-hop band called the Roots. From there, he went on to produce and co-produce hit records for many artists, including Justin Timberlake, 50 Cent, Chamillionaire, Christina Aguilera, Beyoncé, Dr. Dre, Paris Hilton, Ice Cube, Method Man, Kelis, and Jessica Simpson. According to the *New York Times*, Storch's success rate for producing hit songs means that he earns between $80,000 and $90,000 for every song he produces. His income allows him to finance a luxurious lifestyle that includes multiple Bentleys, a mansion in Miami, and diamond jewelry that he wears as though it were everyday attire. Despite his flashy **persona**, Storch has earned a reputation for shyness, especially compared to some of his fellow hip-hop producers like Pharrell Williams and Kanye West.

Storch produced Chris's single "Run It!" and he also helped Chris put together his debut album. With Storch's expertise and fame giving him a boost, it's no wonder that Chris's debut took the music world by storm.

Others

Chris Brown has also gotten some help from other musicians, including the Underdogs and Dr. Dre. One of the most important musicians in Chris's young career, though, is Usher. Even before Chris signed his first record deal, Usher called him up and gave him some advice.

On Chris's Web site, he says that he expected Usher to tell him to sign with LA Reid, who had asked Usher to call. Instead, Usher told

Scott Storch produced Chris's debut single and album. Storch's reputation for producing mega-hits for artists such as Justin Timberlake, 50 Cent, and Beyoncé earns him a reported $80,000 to $90,000 for every *song* he produces.

Chris welcomes the opportunity to perform with other musicians. In this photo, he is seen performing at music mogul Clive Davis's pre-Grammy party in 2006 with (left to right) Alicia Keys, Natalie Cole, and Fantasia Barrino.

Chris, "I'm not going to tell you who to go with. I'm just saying whatever decision you make, be sure it's the right decision for you."

Chris was overwhelmed that Usher had called him; after all, he said, "He was the one who the youngsters looked up to. I know that we, in the dancing and singing world, looked up to him." Chris took the opportunity to ask Usher what he's learned from his own career.

"You get out of it what you put into it," Usher told him.

Chris has taken that advice to heart, and he's giving his career his all. And in return, fame and fortune have come his way.

SANAA LATHAN ON THOSE DENZEL RUMORS

PLUS: DWYANE WADE / FLOETRY / BUN B / THE BOONDOCKS

VIBe

TRAVEL SPECIAL
4 HOT SPOTS FOR 2006!

CHRIS BROWN
THE FUTURE OF R&B

ALICIA KEYS
GIVES UP THE GOODS pg. 42

REMY MA
AS NASTY AS SHE WANTS TO BE

U.S. $3.99/CAN $5.50
FEBRUARY 2006

www.vibe.com

You know you've made it big when you're on the cover of *Vibe* magazine. Chris made the cover for the February 2006 issue. With a hit single and album, worldwide fame, and earning money of his own, Chris isn't a typical teen.

4

Fame and Fortune

t's not every sixteen-year-old who gets his face on the cover of *Vibe* magazine. And not many teenagers can afford to buy their mothers a Ford Expedition with their very own money. And most adolescents can go Christmas shopping at the mall without being mobbed by fans. But all that is the reality for Chris Brown.

Adjustments

Being a star takes some getting used, no matter how much fun it might be. Nearly overnight, Chris's entire life has changed. He told Virgin.net how different his life is now.

> **"I remember just last year I was in 10th grade school trying out for basketball practice. They knew I was doing my music, though. It kinda hurt when I went back and everybody was like 'Yo Chris!' all of a sudden and wanting to know me. When I go into town they're like 'Oh Chris Brown, Chris Brown.' I'm glad they are proud of me but I just want people to be themselves and not phoney."**

Fans

If being famous is an adjustment, it's still a fun ego trip. What teenage boy wouldn't be excited to have hoards of girls pulling him off stage and chasing his car?

"I love it," Chris told MTV. "I'm a fan groupie. I love catering to the fans. Even if I see a group of girls outside, I love sticking my head out the window like, 'Yo, hi!'"

Chris's manager, Tina Davis, described to Pollster some of the attention Chris is getting from the opposite sex:

> **When his backdrop went off, the girls just started screaming and continued to scream from the time he got on the stage until the time he left. We'd be driving down the freeway on our way to the next venue and people would be blowing their horns trying to pull us over to sign autographs. After every show we'd have to get a police escort because the girls wouldn't let the bus go.**

Chris never expected the level of fan response he's receiving, but he's definitely having fun with it. "Oh, it's crazy all the time," he told Pollster. "It's even better in the countries that speak other languages. If they know the words to your song and they speak another language, that's telling me a lot—that I'm doing a good job."

Money

With his record sales still climbing, Chris has a pretty healthy bank balance these days. When Virgin.net asked him what he does with his money, he proudly held up his diamond-encrusted chain and watch. Then he added:

> **I've put it in a trust fund but I get a little something. With my first pay I bought my mum a house in New Jersey. I don't go crazy but I like to buy a little something here and there. I also collect sneakers—I like to customize them with my own art.**

From buying a house to buying sneakers whenever he wants, Chris is enjoying the chance to spend some of his money. What sixteen-year-old wouldn't?

Chris has been a fan favorite almost since the beginning. Everywhere he goes, Chris is greeted by screaming fans, especially girls. And he loves it! Here fans are eager to get a touch from their favorite star during a 2006 concert.

Getting an Education

Chris may be a teen idol with plenty of money, but that doesn't mean he can totally escape some of the restrictions that go along with being a kid. When he's on the road, his **entourage** includes not only his backup dancers, his manager, and all the other professional support he needs, but his mom and a tutor as well.

Tina Davis believes it's a great learning experience for a young adult, but in an interview with MTV, she stressed that none of them forget how important Chris's more traditional education is as well. He goes to school with his tutor every morning, including Saturdays and Sundays. "You know," Tina said,

Chris and his mother, Joyce Hawkins, are very close; Chris calls her his mentor. She helps guide his life, making sure that he continues his education. Though he respects his mother, however, Chris doesn't want anyone thinking he's a little kid.

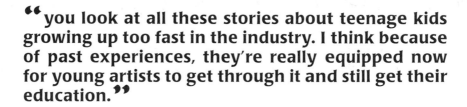

❝you look at all these stories about teenage kids growing up too fast in the industry. I think because of past experiences, they're really equipped now for young artists to get through it and still get their education.❞

Chris added his take on his studies: "It keeps me grounded, definitely. I'm real excited for the most part but really anxious and just trying to see what's happening next after everything I do."

When Virgin.net asked Chris who he looks to for guidance as he navigates the challenges of being both a teenager and a star, he answered, "God, and my manager. I look up to her and she's my guidance. My mum is also my mentor."

Proving Himself

Just because Chris respects his mom's advice, though, doesn't mean he wants anyone to mistake him for a little kid. He told Virgin.net that he gets pretty annoyed when people don't respect him as a professional.

❝You need a certain level of maturity in the music business. I'm cool to play around but when it's time to do business like doing the shows people are like 'ahhh, he's just a little kid.' It can get frustrating as they should have the same respect for me that I have for them. I'm not saying I'm grown up but look at me like an equal. I'm still a 16-year-old kid playing video games and things but I do that in my own time so I'm going to be mature when it's time to be mature.❞

With so many opportunities coming his way, both within and outside the music industry, Chris Brown is doing his best to prove not only his talent but his maturity.

Chris isn't content to be known only as a musical artist. He is taking the opportunities music has opened for him to explore other options available to him, both inside and outside the music world.

‹5›

Outside the Music World

As a young new star, new opportunities are opening up for Chris all the time—and not all of them are in the music world. In March 2006, he also had the chance to try his hand at acting on a UPN sitcom. And on top of that, he's finding out that fame offers him occasions to be a role model for others as well.

Acting

Chris was excited to have the chance to have a **cameo** appearance on one of his own favorite sitcoms, *One on One*. But when the time came to say his lines, he had to overcome some nerves. Standing up on a stage with a mic is one thing; Chris has that covered. But that doesn't mean he wasn't nervous when it came time say his dialogue on the soundstage.

Chris told MTV, "I was a little nervous. There was some stumbling sometimes, but I got through it. Everybody does that and it gets easier."

In the episode, Chris plays himself. After he performs at a party, he tries to put the moves on a girl—but he gets turned down because of his age. Nineteen-year-old Kyla Pratt, who plays Breanna, the girl Chris tries to pick up on the episode, told MTV, "Chris approaches me, and I go, 'OK, you're cute, but you're *sixteen*.' Then he's like, 'It's OK, we can still get something going. You ain't afraid of a little jail time, are you?'"

Chris added, "The Chris you're talking to right now isn't trying to be too suave or too gangsta, but here I had to play the role of the star, like, 'Hey, baby, how you doing?' Like I'm the *stuff*. That's not me at all, so I had to be a lot smoother."

Chris's experience on *One on One* gave him the chance to pick up some pointers from singer Ray J, who stars as D-Mack on the show, and also from singer Marques Houston, who was acting in his own UPN sitcom, *Cuts*, next door to the *One on One* studio. Afterward, Ray J told MTV:

"Chris is a natural. You can just tell in his style and his confidence as an artist that . . . he knows what he wants in life and he shows that on the set. It's really all about having fun and I think he displayed that today in a really positive way."

Houston added that his advice to Chris had been "to do his thing."

Kyla Pratt put in her thoughts on Chris's performance in the studio:

"When he first came in, he seemed a little shy and was talking a little low. [Eventually] he got comfortable with us and got all loud, so everything turned out great. I think he has a little future in the acting business."

Chris has seen what other musicians, especially his role model Usher, have been able to accomplish in the acting world, and he believes that for him, television is just the beginning. From there, he wants to move on to the big screen. He's been looking through a stack of scripts, he told MTV, including a couple of dance flicks and a drama.

"I'm just looking right now, trying to see which one will really fit me," he said.

Acting is just one area that Chris is exploring. In 2006, he made his acting debut playing himself on the television show *One on One*. Here he is seen with his costar, series regular Kyla Pratt.

"My dream role is just to be like myself, [but in a role involving] action or basketball or fighting. Not saying I *like* the fighting, but it would be a great experience for me to be able to do something out of the box that's still in my origin."

Chris has at least got his foot in Hollywood's door: he landed a song on the soundtrack of Usher's movie, *In the Mix*. When Chris had the chance to work with Usher on the soundtrack, Chris was nearly overwhelmed. He told MTV:

Usher (left, in a scene from the movie *In the Mix*) has been a major influence on Chris's career. Chris had the opportunity to record a song on the soundtrack for *In the Mix*. Chris wouldn't mind following in Usher's acting steps as well.

"To see him face-to-face, I was like, 'OK, Chris, it's gonna be all right, just chill out right quick. You about to do the song, man, don't be no punk.' 'Cause I was like, 'Yo, that's Usher! That's Usher,' like going crazy at first. Then as I got to know him, he was a regular person just like me. Working [together] was great—the chemistry was there.**"**

Being a Role Model

Lots of hip-hop musicians are doing their part to make the world a better place, including Chris's hero, Usher. One of Usher's biggest dreams is to be able to give inner-city kids the same opportunities that

Chris is using his success and fame to do good works. In 2005, he participated in *Today*'s Annual Toy Drive, collecting gifts for underprivileged children in New York City. This is just one way for Chris to be a role model for kids—and adults.

he had when he was growing up. "A lot of negativity comes through life for a lot of minorities," he told *Rolling Stone*. "I try to be positive and I try to act as positive role model." In 2005, Usher also opened Camp New Look in Atlanta, Georgia. This summer camp for minority youth is designed to help talented kids achieve their dreams. Usher realizes how fortunate his own life has been—and he wants to do his part to continue to pass along that good fortune to young people who are coming up within the black community.

Chris is still pretty young and his career is brand new—but that doesn't stop him from doing his best to follow Usher's example. In 2005, he received a nomination from the NAACP for his positive contribution to the African American community. The NAACP followed up the nomination in February 2006 with an award for Outstanding New Artist. The NAACP isn't the only organization to be impressed with Chris. He also won the MTV TRL Award and a *Soul Train* award, also for Outstanding New Artist.

Chris Brown proves that kids can excel; he's a role model for others his age. That reputation is one of the things that landed him a guest performance on Nickelodeon's *Kids' Choice Awards* in April 2006. He, Bow Wow, and Pink enjoyed the chance to rock the young crowd. Marjorie Cohn, Executive Vice President, Development and Original Programming, said of the show: "These kid favorites can't wait to shed their Hollywood image for a night of un-stuffy slime-filled fun. It's a real affirmation of kid power."

Kid power is what Chris's life is all about.

The Sky's the Limit

As Chris headed out on his first tour in spring of 2006, he described what his life is like to the *Seattle Intelligencer*:

> **"It's been hectic. It's been total chaos. I've been on the go for like two weeks straight. I had to go to school, I had to do a lot of interviews, I had to perform and still rehearse. We do long rehearsals. I have to make sure the band is doing the right song, and I gotta make sure they know the songs. I gotta learn like four or five routines with different choreography for each song. It's been hectic, but at the same time, it's what I live for."**

Though early in his career, Chris has already won recognition for his work and contributions to society. The NAACP nominated him for an award for his good works in 2005. In 2006, he won the Outstanding New Artist award at the NAACP Image Awards.

In 2006, Chris went out on his first tour. Fans all over the country now had the opportunity to see him perform in person. Although it has been hectic, Chris loves it—and the fans love him!

Touring doesn't take up all Chris's time. He also works on his next album, which goes into production in October 2006. This time around, he wants to work with Scott Storch again, as well as hip-hop superstars Kanye West and Pharrell Williams.

Chris has also received the honor of being "punk'd." *Punk'd* is MTV's hidden-camera, practical-joke series. On Chris's episode, which aired in April 2006, Chris Brown took his mom and manager to a restaurant; when his mom got sick from the salad, the waiter accused him of being rude and told the manager he was causing problems. Chris handled it with good grace.

Being punk'd is the least of the surprises in Chris's life. Amazing opportunities have come his way. Who knows where his talent, determination, and hard work will take him next?

1600s–1800s	People bring slaves to the United States.
1920s	Jazz becomes a popular music form in the United States.
1931	Sam Cooke is born.
1940s	The blues combine with jazz to become rhythm and blues.
1956	Sam Cooke releases his first pop single.
1958	Michael Jackson is born.
1960s	Gospel and R&B combine into soul music.
	The Jackson 5 becomes a household word.
1970s	DJ Kool Herc pioneers the use of breaks, isolations, and repeats using two turntables.
	Break dancing emerges at parties and in public places in New York City.
	Graffiti artist Vic makes his mark in New York, sparking the act of tagging.
	Hip-hop as a cultural movement begins in the Bronx, New York City.
1979	Donnie Hathaway, considered by many the greatest soul musician of the 1970s, commits suicide.
1980s	Anita Baker helps define a classy, refined brand of romantic soul.
1980s	Hip-hop spreads to small-town rural America.
1988	Hip-hop record sales hit $100 million.
1989	Chris Brown is born on May 5 in Tappahannock, Virginia.
2005	Chris releases his debut single, "Run It!"
	Chris releases his first album, *Chris Brown*.
	Chris is nominated for an NAACP award.

2006   Chris receives an MTV TRL award.

Chris receives a *Soul Train* award.

Chris embarks on his first tour.

Chris Brown is certified platinum.

Chris receives the Outstanding New Artist Award from the NAACP.

Chris makes his television acting debut on TV sitcom *One on One*.

Chris is "punk'd."

Discography
Solo Album
2005   *Chris Brown*

Number-one Single
2005   "Run It"

Selected Television Appearances
2005   *TRL* (MTV)

2006   *Punk'd* (MTV)

   One on One (UPN)

   The Shop (MTV)

   Monster Mix: Hip Hop (MTV)

Awards
2006   MTV TRL Award: Favorite Artist Under 21

   NAACP Image Awards: Outstanding New Artist

   Soul Train Music Awards: Best R&B/Soul or Rap New Artist

   Billboard Awards: Artist of the Year, Male Artist of the Year,
      New Artist of the Year

Books

Baker, Soren. *History of Rap and Hip-Hop.* Farmington Hills, Mich.: Thomson Gale, 2006.

Chang, Jeff, and DJ Kool Herc (Introduction). *Can't Stop, Won't Stop: A History of the Hip-Hop Generation.* New York: St. Martin's Press, 2005.

Lord, Raymond. *Usher.* Broomall, Pa.: Mason Crest Publishers, 2007.

Waters, Rosa. *Hip-Hop: A Short History.* Broomall, Pa.: Mason Crest Publishers, 2007.

Magazines

Cafferty, Leslie. "Chris Brown: This R&B Crooner's Tools of Seduction: Slick Moves, a Velvet Voice, and a Mother Who Just Won't Quit." *Interview,* December 1, 2005.

"CHARTS: 'It' Happens—Chris Brown and Beyonce Will Tell You That." *Entertainment Weekly,* February 24, 2006.

"Heating Up the Charts with Rhythm & Blues." *New York Times Up Front,* November 28, 2005.

Hope, Clover. "Chris Brown." *Billboard,* December 3, 2005.

"Is He the New Usher?" *People,* December 12, 2005.

Web Sites

Aceshowbiz: Chris Brown
www.aceshowbiz.com/celebrity/chris_brown

Chris Brown
www.chrisbrownweb.com

Chris Brown Fan Page
www.popstarplus.com/music_chrisbrown.htm

Chris Brown (singer)
www.danceage.com/biography/sdmc_Chris_Brown_(singer)

"R&B Singer Chris Brown Soars to Top of Charts with Single 'Run It,' and New Debut Album"
www.blacknews.com/pr/chrisbrown101.html

ballads—slow romantic or sentimental songs.

bootleg—unauthorized recording.

cameo—a single brief appearance by a distinguished performer in a movie or play.

choreographer—someone who directs the movements in a dance.

debut—done for the first time.

DJs—people who play recorded music for the entertainment of others; disc jockeys.

emceeing—acting as a master of ceremonies for an event.

entourage—one's attendants.

gospel—highly emotional evangelical vocal music that originated among African Americans in the South.

inductee—someone who is admitted as a member to an organization.

minority—a portion of the population with characteristics different from most.

persona—an individual's social shell.

platinum—indicating that a single has sold one million copies or an album or CD two million units.

secular—not relating to religion.

spontaneous—done without planning, on the spur of the moment.

testimonies—public professions of Christian beliefs or faith.

versatile—changing readily.

page

2: Jive Records/NMI

8: Zuma Press/Lora Voigt

11: Reuters/Mike Hutchings

12: PictureArts/OBrien Productions

14: KRT/NMI

15: BSIP/Jack Griffin

16: Piotr Redlinski/Sipa Press

19: Zuma Press/Lora Voigt

20: Jemal Countess/WireImage

22: Michelle Feng/NMI

25: Mark Cardwell/Reuters

26: Hulton Archive/Getty Images

28: Lionel Hahn/Abaca Press/KRT

30: KRT/John Collier

31: Michelle Feng/NMI

32: Kevin Mazur/WireImage

34: AP Photo/Jennifer Graylock

38: Fashion Wire Daily/ Maria Ramirez

39: Laura Farr/AdMedia

40: Michelle Feng/NMI

43: Zuma Press/Jason Moore

44: Kathy Hutchins/Hutchins Photo

46: Zuma Press/Jerome Ware

49: Randy Tepper/UPN/ Everett Collection

50: Lions Gate Films/NMI

51: Gregg Snodgrass/London Entertainment/Splash News

53: UPI Photo/Jim Ruymen

54: Zuma Press/Jason Moore

Front cover: Zuma Press/Lisa O' Connor
Back cover: Christian Zeise/WENN

James Hooper grew up to the sound of drumbeats. His brother, a drummer, rapped and tapped on any surface he could find, and James gained a love of rhythm. Although James pursued a career in writing rather than music, he has never lost his appreciation for his brother's world. James has written previously for newspapers and magazines, and welcomes any chance to describe the world of music with words.